Forest of Dean & Wye Valley Travel Guide

Sightseeing, Hotel, Restaurant & Shopping Highlights

Thomas Austin

Copyright © 2014, Astute Press
All Rights Reserved.

No part of this publication may be reproduced, stored in a retrieval system, or transmitted, in any form or by any means without the prior written permission of the publisher, nor be otherwise circulated in any form of binding or cover other than that in which it is published and without similar condition being imposed on the subsequent purchaser.

If there are any errors or omissions in copyright acknowledgements the publisher will be pleased to insert the appropriate acknowledgement in any subsequent printing of this publication.

Although we have taken all reasonable care in researching this book we make no warranty about the accuracy or completeness of its content and disclaim all liability arising from its use

Table of Contents

Forest of Dean & the Wye Valley 5
   Location & Orientation 6
   Climate & When to Visit 8

Sightseeing Highlights 9
   Forest of Dean 9
   Chepstow (Welsh: Cas-Gwent) 11
   Caerleon (Welsh: Caerllion) 12
   Tintern (Welsh: Tyndyrn) 13
   Abergavenny (Welsh: Y Fenni) 15
   Hereford 16
   Monmouth (Welsh: Trefynwy) 17
   Ross-on-Wye 19
   Usk (Welsh: Brynbuga) 20
   Gloucester 21

Recommendations for the Budget Traveller 24
   Places to Stay 24
      Hotel Ibis Gloucester 24
      Castle View Hotel 25
      Riverside Hotel 25
      Munstone House 26
      Premier Inn 27
   Places to Eat 27
      Warwick's Country Pub & Eatery 27
      The Three Salmons 28
      Na Lampang 29
      N68 Bistro 29
      Shangri-La 30
   Places to Shop 30
      Eastgate Shopping Centre 30
      Stella Books 31
      Labels Outlet Shopping 31
      Ross Garden Store 32
      Gloucestershire Arts & Crafts Centre 32

FOREST OF DEAN & THE WYE VALLEY TRAVEL GUIDE

Forest of Dean & the Wye Valley

The Forest of Dean in the Wye Valley is an ancient forest that was once the hunting grounds of King Henry V (born in nearby Monmouth) where he honed the skills that enabled his army to win the historic battle against the French at Agincourt. This is also where William Wordsworth walked and conceived of poetry that has been loved by generations.

The landscape is dotted with small towns that have been around for centuries. Opportunities abound for outdoor enthusiasts, whether on the rivers, walking in the hills or exploring in the forest.

Archaeological digs have provided evidence to show that the region has been inhabited since Mesolithic times. The region marked one of the westernmost reaches of the Roman Empire in Britain, and the forest itself was protected as a hunting ground by the Roman government – a protection it would enjoy through the Tudor period.

In more recent times, the area became known for industry – most notably coal mining, metallurgy and forestry. There are several sites that enjoy international protection for their role at the beginning of the Industrial Revolution. This took its toll on the forest which shrunk in size over the centuries. Today, however, the Forest of Dean and the Wye Valley have been designated as Areas of Outstanding Natural Beauty, which affords them a degree of protection from the threat of redevelopment.

The region straddles the border between England and Wales, and has seen periods of both tension and cooperation between the two countries. Today, visitors will cross between the two countries almost without noticing. You'll enjoy trying to master the pronunciation of the unusual Welsh place names.

Official signs include both the Welsh and English name for a place – and sometimes the two names bear no resemblance to one another.

Location & Orientation

The Wye Valley takes its name from the River Wye that straddles England and Wales. In Wales it crosses the county of Monmouthshire, and in England it extends into Gloucestershire and Herefordshire.

The Forest of Dean is located predominantly in Gloucestershire. It sits on a plateau bordered by the River Wye, the River Severn and the city of Gloucester.

Given the number of small villages and towns, as well as remote locations within the forest, the easiest way to get around is by car. If you will travel by railway to the region, and then hire a car for the duration of your trip, there are major railway stations at Abergavenny, Chepstow, Lydney and Gloucester. Similarly, there are National Express coach stations in Newent, Chepstow, Ross-on-Wye, Monmouth and Gloucester.

For those who'll be entering the UK by plane, the closest airports are Bristol, Cardiff and Birmingham. All three are within a 90-minute driving radius. The London airports and Manchester airport are also viable options despite being further away.

There is a £3.50 parking fee in the Forestry Commission car parks. An annual Forestry Commission Discovery Pass can be purchased for £20 that will allow you to park in Forestry Commission car parks for a year, and it also gives additional perks and discounts on related services.

Please see their website at:
http://www.forestry.gov.uk/pass.

Climate & When to Visit

The region experiences a mild oceanic climate. The hottest months are July and August when temperatures range from 13°C to 23°C (55°F to 75°F). This is also the driest time of year with an average rainfall of around two inches/month. Winter temperatures are typically at their coldest in December and January when they range from 3°C to 8°C (37°F to 46°F). The wettest months are in the spring and fall.

Many of the towns host Christmas markets that attract tourists during the winter.

The stunning natural beauty of the area is present at all times of year, so the best time to visit really depends on when you're free to travel and your personal preferences. You'll find there's much to discover in any season.

Sightseeing Highlights

Forest of Dean

Visitors to the Forest of Dean will enjoy a large array of outdoor activities. Popular hiking trails include the **Wye Valley Walk**, which runs from Chepstow to Plylimon in central Wales and passes through rugged terrain, much of it historically relevant. **Offa's Dyke Path** follows the earthen barrier built by King Offa in the 8th century – which marks, roughly, the border of England and Wales today. The Wysis Way bisects the Forest of Dean, passing through some stunning terrain, and goes through Gloucester into the Cotswolds.

Many will enjoy cycling throughout the region. There are bike trails for all levels, from those suitable for families with children to those for more adventurous mountain bikers. The **Family Cycle trail** follows the former Severn and Wye railway on a ten-mile circle through the forest. Mountain bike enthusiasts will find trails of different grades, and even a set of skills loops to help you develop your abilities and control.

If you aren't traveling with your own bike, you can hire one from Pedalabikeaway Cycle Center (http://www.pedalabikeaway.co.uk/), Dean Forest Cycles (http://www.deanforestcycles.co.uk/) and Forest Bikes (http://www.forestbikes.com/).

If you'd like to explore the Wye Valley from the vantage point of the river that gives the region its name, you'll find any number of canoe and kayak rental shops in the towns that line the Wye's riverbanks. Monmouth Canoe's rates start at £20 for a half-day (http://www.monmouthcanoe.co.uk/river-wye-canoeing/). For £55, Way2Go Adventures in Symond's Wat offers guided half- and full-day trips along the river – and have sea-kayaking tours.
http://www.way2goadventures.co.uk/).

There are also places to rock climb, caves to explore with trained spelunkers, a number of zip-line courses to explore the forest canopy and more. Check out the regions website for more details:
http://www.visitforestofdean.co.uk/discover/Things%20to%20do/t-1553%7C/

Chepstow (Welsh: Cas-Gwent)

This charming town sits at the lower end of the Wye Valley and serves as an unofficial "entrance" to the region. It's castle was the first built after the Norman Conquest and has watched over the entrance to the Severn River ever since. The town grew up around the castle and has been an important port and market town for almost 1000 years.

Chepstow was once a part of the Wye Tour (at the dawn of the modern age of tourism). Chepstow has long attracted visitors from all parts of Britain in search of romantic landscapes.

The **Chepstow Museum** (Gwy House, Bridge Street, Tel: 01291 625981) recalls the town's history, and the history of the Wye Tour and its influence on the region. It is located very close to the castle.

The **Old Wye Bridge** was built in the early 19th century and is an important landmark today. It is notable for its beautiful cast iron construction – which is difficult to maintain given that it spans the Severn at a point where the river's tide at times rises and falls by 40 feet! The bridge crosses the border between England and Wales. You can stand in the middle of the bridge with one foot in England and the other in Wales.

Caerleon (Welsh: Caerllion)

Not far from Chepstow is the small town of Caerleon. This town is of importance historically as the site of a permanent Roman legionary fortress – one of only three in Britain. Unlike most of the UK's Roman ruins Caerleon's are special due to their size...and because many archaeologists and historians think it may be King Arthur's seat of power. That's right: Caerleon may well be **Camelot**!

Caerleon was known to the Romans in its day as *Isca Augusta*, and it was the westernmost outpost of the Roman Empire in Britannia, a fortress that was inhabited for over 200 years, possibly as late as 380 AD.

Take a look at the remains of the iconic amphitheatre (the most intact in the UK) that once seated 60,000 spectators (almost seven times the number of the current population!). Portions of the fortress wall still survive (despite centuries of locals having taken the stones for their own buildings). The barracks are the best-preserved Roman barracks in Europe.

If you'd like to put the town's ancient sites into some context, visit the **National Roman Legion Museum**. Its permanent exhibition includes many artefacts discovered in the area. It also features rooms reconstructed to look like they would have appeared to the Roman soldiers who inhabited them. There is also a **Roman Baths Museum** where you can see the ruins of the thermal baths where the Roman soldiers would have cleaned up and relaxed after a day of training.

The Arthurian connections trace back to Geoffrey of Monmouth, whose 12th century opus, *The History of the Kings of Britain*, is the first to specify that Caerleon was a place connected to King Arthur. The fact that Geoffrey wrote his book 600 years after the death of Arthur and archaeological evidence doesn't support the theory hasn't stopped subsequent authors from considering Caerleon the site of Camelot. The fact is, there isn't much evidence to disprove the theory either – and it's not hard to imagine the amphitheatre as the famed roundtable. Even if it's not a table exactly, it's still a circular gathering place – perhaps *table* was just a metaphor?

Caerleon hosts an **arts festival** every July. It features tree sculptures from around the world that are displayed all over the town. The festival happens in conjunction with the annual Roman legion battle reenactment that takes place in the amphitheatre.

Tintern (Welsh: Tyndyrn)

William Wordsworth was a notable walker of the Wye Tour. He liked it so much, in fact, that five years later he walked it again with his sister (and best friend), Dorothy. The poems that he wrote during that time period found their way into *Lyrical Ballads*, his collaboration with Samuel Taylor Coleridge. The book marked a dramatic shift in the content and structure of poetry and it ushered in the British Romantic era.

One poem in particular, "Lines written a few miles above Tintern Abbey" – commonly known as **"Tintern Abbey"** – has been taught in schools and universities all over the Anglophone world and is what put the Wye Valley on the map. The ruined abbey exists today in much the same condition as it did when the Wordsworths visited in the late 18th century.

When the Cistercian abbey was built in the 12th century it was the first of its kind in Wales. The abbey saw 400 years of monastic life before Henry VIII dissolved the monasteries and liquidated their assets in the 16th century. The lord of Chepstow sold off lead from the abbey's roof shortly thereafter, putting in motion the centuries of decay that would follow.

Although the abbey is the most famous site in the area, you'll also want to see the **Abbey Mill**. Although it's hard to imagine today in it's bucolic setting, Tintern was once a major industrial area and an important producer of bronzeware. The Abbey Mill is a testament to that era with its ancient water wheel. Today the mill is home to a variety of craft studios and shops where visitors can browse the work of local artists and artisans.

Abergavenny (Welsh: Y Fenni)

Abergavenny is sometimes referred to as "The Gateway to Wales," which is disputable since it doesn't even sit along the border. It is, however, the indisputable gateway to the **Brecon Beacons national park**. The Brecon Beacons mountain range is rocky and stark. The first time you see the mountains, you will begin to feel that the landscape has suddenly become less English and more definitively Welsh – which gives merit to Abergavenny's nickname.

The Brecon Beacons National Park edges up against the Wye Valley and the park has been designated an International Dark-Sky Reserve – which is to say, a place with so little light pollution that you can still experience darkness as our ancestors before the 20th century would have experienced it.

Abergavenny is famous for its **food festival** (http://abergavennyfoodfestival.com/), which The Guardian has deemed as important to the food world as Cannes is to the film world. The festival takes place every September, and if you visit you'll find hundreds of different food stalls, cookery classes, talks, debates, wine tastings, etc. It's held in one of the major market halls in Wales, which is worth a visit at any time of year. Here you'll find an antiques market, a crafts market and a flea market in addition to the daily farmers' market.

Abergavenny has a reputation as a foodie's paradise and you will find plenty of good places to eat no matter what time of year you visit. You can learn about the town's history by visiting its museum, which is set in the ruins of a Norman castle – one of the finest examples of a motte and bailey castle in Britain.

You're also a short drive away from **Blaenavon, a UNESCO World Heritage Site**. Its ironworks had such an impact on metallurgy that similar foundries followed and the Industrial Revolution was begun.

Hereford

Hereford sits along the River Wye on the English-side of the border with Wales. The first thing you'll see towering over the Hereford landscape is its 11th century **Norman Cathedral**. Here you can see the *Mappa Mundi* – a map of the world as it was depicted by a 13th century cartographer. It's the largest complete medieval map and is very important to historians.

You can also visit the cathedral's library. During the medieval period all books were manuscripts (by the Latin definition: *written by hand*). A manuscript as long as the Bible took an incredibly long time to create and was therefore very valuable. In ancient times, books were chained to pedestals to prevent theft as you can see at the library. The cathedral library is one of the largest, best-preserved chained medieval libraries. Here you can see beautiful illuminated manuscripts of the Gospels from the Saxon period.

After spending an afternoon learning about the Middle Ages in the cathedral, you'll be ready for a drink. Hereford is home to the Bulmers Cider company – maker of Bulmers and Strongbow ciders (among others). Hereford is also home to **The Cider Museum** (http://www.cidermuseum.co.uk/ at Pomona Place; Tel: 01432 354207) and **King Offa Distillery** where you can learn all about the history and process of making cider.

Monmouth (Welsh: Trefynwy)

This busy market town sits in the heart of the Wye Valley and lends its name to the surrounding county of Monmouthshire. Although most of the architecture is noticeably Georgian, this was a very important town in medieval times and there are traces of this history still to be found.

Most prominent is the **Monnow Bridge** with its medieval stone gate that is fully intact – the only one of its kind that remains in Great Britain. Its Norman castle, now in ruins, will be of interest to devotees of history and Shakespeare. It was the birthplace of Prince Hal, later King Henry V. The castle also houses a regimental museum.

Also of interest to Shakespeare enthusiasts: the medieval historian Geoffrey of Monmouth is from here. His *History of the Kings of Britain* provided the source material for several of Shakespeare's plays as well as the earliest tales of King Arthur.

Moving ahead in time, **Monmouth's Shire Hall** is an elegant Georgian courthouse and county administrative centre. It's important in modern British history as the site where leaders of the Chartist movement were put on trial in the 1840s. Rulings on this populist movement reverberated through the country and had lasting effects on British democracy.

The **Kymin**, a Georgian banquet hall, sits on the outskirts of town and is the perfect place for you to bring a picnic lunch. Its location atop a wooded hill presents the visitor with incredible views of the surrounding Monmouthshire countryside. Admiral Lord Nelson brought his mistress, Lady Hamilton, here and described it as the most beautiful place he'd ever seen.

Speaking of Nelson, the **Monmouth Museum** has such a large collection of his memorabilia that it is often mistakenly referred to as the **Nelson Museum**. Their collection contains many of his personal letters and his fighting sword.

One of Monmouth's favorite sons of the last 150 years is Charles Rolls. A dashing, aristocratic adventurer, Rolls was an early automobile enthusiast, balloonist and one of Britain's first licensed airplane pilots. He was also, sadly, the first Briton to die in an airplane accident in 1910 at the age of 32. Although his life was cut short, at the time of his death he held the world record for the longest balloon flight and he was the first person to make a non-stop flight across the English Channel. Most importantly, however, is the legacy he left to the automobile world: in 1906 he and his friend Henry Royce founded the Rolls-Royce company.

You can visit Rolls' home, **The Hendre**, which is the best-preserved Victorian manse in Monmouthshire. If you're a golfer, you might want to consider playing at the **Rolls of Monmouth Golf Club** located on the grounds surrounding the house. Visit their website for more information (http://www.therollsgolfclub.co.uk/).

Ross-on-Wye

The picturesque town of Ross-on-Wye sits on the northern edge of the Forest of Dean and is a good place to base yourself to explore the Wye Valley. An easy way to do this is to take a boat cruise. **Wye Valley Cruises** (http://www.wyenot.com/wyecruises01.htm; Symonds Yat Leisure Park, Symonds Yat West; Tel: 07721 895346) launch from the nearby small village of Symonds Yat West and take you on a leisurely excursion down the river. You can also arrange to hire canoes and kayaks from here.

Back in town, take a look at the **market hall**. Built in the 1650s, this red sandstone structure sits in the middle of the town centre and is still the site of a bustling market scene as well as antique stores and artisan boutiques.

St. Mary's Church is built of the same rusty-coloured sandstone as the market hall, and you can see its towering spire from the moment you enter the town. The church is over 700 years old and contains some beautiful medieval sculpted tombs. Outside be sure to take a moment of contemplation before the Plague Cross. Erected in 1637, it stands as a monument to the more than 300 townspeople who died of the plague that year and who were buried hastily – without much ceremony and without coffins – nearby in a plague pit.

Next to the church you'll find the **Prospect**, a lovely garden park that offers some excellent views of the town and environs.

Across the river from Ross you'll find **Wilton Castle**. A popular ruined Norman fortress that is covered in ivy and roses. A walk through its gardens makes for a romantic afternoon spent in a fairy tale setting.

Goodrich Castle, in nearby Goodrich, is of a similar age and in a similar condition as Wilton but is a more imposing structure. Its high walls remind you that castles were built, first and foremost, for defense. This site is maintained by English Heritage and has excellent audio guide to lead you around as you explore.

Usk (Welsh: Brynbuga)

Usk is located on the river of the same name. One of the oldest towns in Wales, this is a quiet town that is known for its horticulturally adept citizens. They've won many awards in the annual **Britain in Bloom competition**, and if you'd like to see why then be sure to visit them in June when the residents open their private gardens to the public. It's a wonderful way to meet some of the locals.

Usk Castle is a ruined Norman fortification, which sits off the beaten path. The entry fee is whatever you care to donate, and their means of counting the number of visitors every day is to have you drop a pebble into a bowl. Once in, you're likely to find yourself as one of very few visitors, so you can enjoy the ruins and the gardens in a quiet ambience.

The **Rural Life Museum** (The Malt Barn, New Market Street, Tel: 01291 673777; http://www.uskmuseum.org/) is a popular attraction. It shows how agriculture changed from the pre-motor times of 1850 to 1950 by displaying hundreds of different tools and machines. Its library is also an impressive collection of books, photographs and records. Before you leave, be sure to get your picture taken with Bessie, a fake-yet-somehow-milkable cow!

Gloucester

Gloucester is a beautiful cathedral and port city located on the Severn. Gloucester straddles two distinct and interesting regions: the Wye Valley and Wales to the west and the ever-charming Cotswolds to the south and east.

Gloucester cathedral dominates the skyline and parts of it have been around since the Saxon era in the 7th century (although most of what you see was built later between the 11th and 15th centuries).

Like most cathedrals and large churches, if you pay attention to the details you'll notice some quirks and eccentricities. Two quirks of note in Gloucester Cathedral are located in its stained glass windows where you can see people playing golf in one of the stained glass windows and a medieval version of football in another. The golf window is particularly puzzling since golf originated in Scotland yet this image is 300 years older.

If you walk around the cloisters and begin to feel like you've entered Hogwarts School of Witchcraft and Wizardry, that's because the cathedral was used extensively in three of the **Harry Potter films**.

After the cathedral, the city is best known for its **Victorian docks**. Although inland, its position on the Severn makes it a perfect river port. A great place to learn about this history is the **Gloucester Waterways Museum**. Once you've learned about the importance of the city as a port during the Victorian era, you can get on the water yourself in one of their many daily canal tours.

Also take a look at **Prinknash Abbey**. Not only do the buildings date from the 11th through the 16th centuries, but there is still an active monastic community living here and following the Rule of St. Benedict – written nearly 1500 years ago. While parts of the monastery are not open to the public, the abbey does welcome visitors to its gardens and it maintains an aviary (with many free-roaming birds) and a deer park.

By comparison with the other towns and villages in the region, Gloucester is quite large and cosmopolitan. It has, therefore, more to offer in terms of nightlife. If you're looking for a fun night on the town you'll find many bars and clubs on Lower Eastgate Street, including Liquid/Diva and The Registry, which are the biggest.

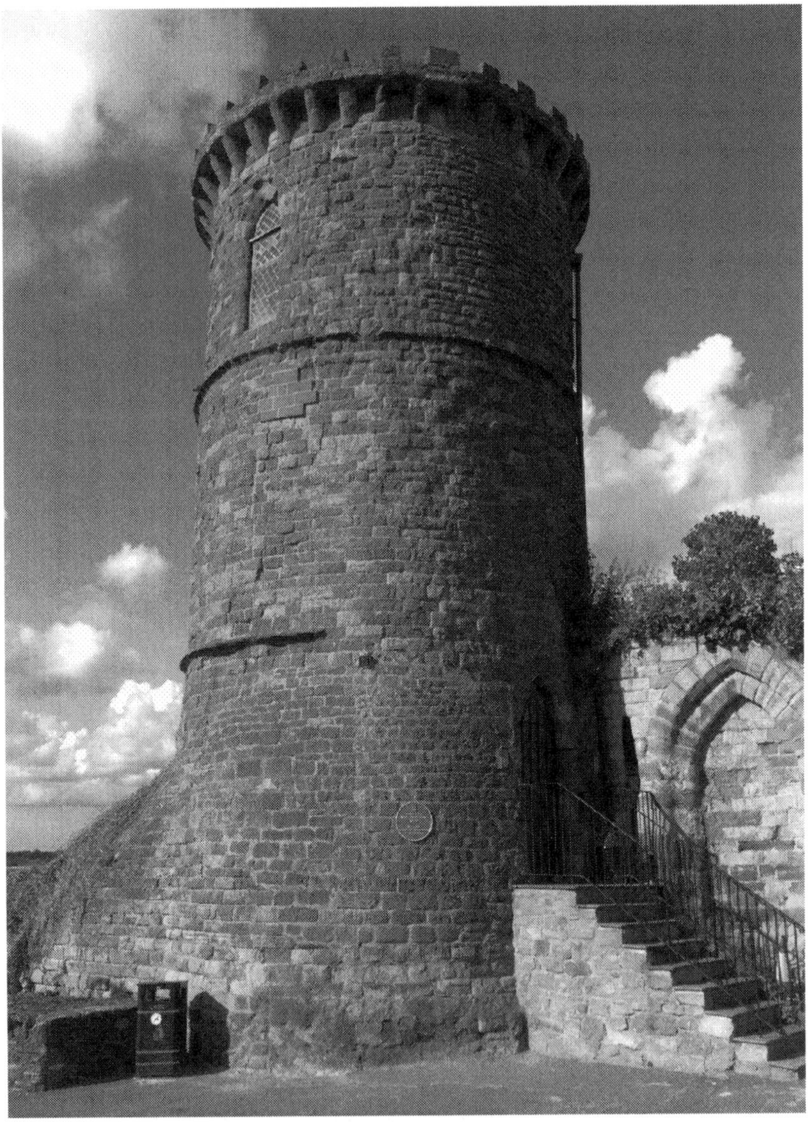

Recommendations for the Budget Traveller

Places to Stay

Hotel Ibis Gloucester

Corinium Ave A417
Gloucester
GL4 3DG
Tel: 01452 623650
http://www.ibis.com/gb/hotel-6900-ibis-gloucester/index.shtml

The Hotel Ibis offers clean, modern rooms at an affordable price (less than £40/night if you book online). If you're driving, you could easily make Gloucester your home base for a few days and travel into the rest of the Wye Valley as a series of day trips. This hotel is located near the city centre, and rooms come equipped with free WiFi, hair dryers and satellite television. There is a restaurant and bar on site.

Castle View Hotel

16 Bridge Street
Chepstow
NP16 5EZ
Tel: 01291 620349
http://www.hotelchepstow.co.uk/

This is a handsome, Tudor house-turned-hotel in Chepstow that enjoys an excellent location directly across from Chepstow Castle. It's a small hotel with only 13 rooms (although the 13th is numbered 14…just to be safe), so be sure to book ahead. If you stay here you'll enjoy seeing the murals and tapestries that have been in the house since the 1600s. It boasts an excellent restaurant and a garden pub. A single room can be booked through their website for £45. Online rates for a double room can be found around £60.

Riverside Hotel

Cinderhill Street
Monmouth
NP25 5EY
Tel: 01600 715577
http://www.riversidehotelmonmouth.co.uk/

This hotel used to be a Victorian coaching inn, but today it's somewhat more elegant and comfortable.

Its 19 rooms vary in size and shape, but all come equipped with Free WiFi access and bathrooms en suite. The hotel restaurant serves both full English and Welsh breakfasts, and visitors can enjoy a quiet evening in the residents bar or a louder, more energetic night watching your favorite team at the hotel's sports bar. Rooms are available for under £60 online, and if you visit the hotel's website you'll find they frequently post special package deals.

Munstone House

Munstone
Hereford
HR1 3AH
Tel: 01432 267122
http://www.munstonehouse.com/index.html

This beautiful country house hotel ought to cost much more than the £50-60 they charge per night (which includes a full English breakfast). Located just outside of central Hereford, this hotel offers the visitor beautiful grounds to walk around with fantastic views of the surrounding countryside. Rooms are spacious and luxurious and come with free WiFi. This is a small hotel with just a few rooms, so book ahead to guarantee your place.

Premier Inn

Ledbury Road
Ross-on-Wye
HR9 7QJ
Tel: 08715 278944
http://www.premierinn.com/en/hotel/ROSTRA/ross-on-wye

This chain offers consistent quality at an affordable price. They offer large, comfortable beds, free WiFi, a television with over 80 channels, bathrooms en suite with hair dryers. This location has a Beefeater restaurant on site. The price for a basic room without breakfast or extra frills is £29, so you really can't beat it. It should be noted, however, that this particular location does not have air conditioner units in the rooms – something to remember if you're traveling in July or August.

Places to Eat

Warwick's Country Pub & Eatery

Llantillio Crossenny, Abergavenny, NP7 8TL
Tel: 01600 780227
http://warwickspub.blogspot.com/

Warwick's Country Pub is a great place to go for both traditional British cuisine and a local pub atmosphere.

Located in Abergavenny, halfway to Monmouth, you might want to make this a stop on your way between these two cities. Owners Sue and Alan will give you a warm welcome and give you tips and ideas about other things to see and do in the immediate area. Check out their blog for events at the pub itself – this place is a very active member of its community. Menu items range from £5-£18.

The Three Salmons

Bridge Street
Usk
NP15 1RY
Tel: 01291 672133
http://www.threesalmons.co.uk/restaurant/

The Three Salmons team cooks with produce grown in the chef's garden behind the building and only uses lamb and beef raised in the area. Traditional Welsh fare using local Welsh ingredients. And you can wash it all down with a pint from their selection of locally brewed ales and ciders. Although steaks can cost over £20, most items on their menu are less than £14, so you're getting great quality at a great price. The restaurant is conveniently located in the center of Usk.

Na Lampang

12 Kingsholm Road
Gloucester
Tel: 01452 382970
http://nalampang.weebly.com/home.html

Na Lampang is a highly regarded Thai restaurant in Gloucester. The cuisine is largely from Northern Thailand, which is known for being less spicy than the south. All dishes are made fresh (with ingredients grown in the restaurant's own garden), and the restaurant has a welcoming atmosphere. Most curries, stir-fries and noodle dishes are under £8; specialties and fish are all under £13. This restaurant has developed a following with a regular clientele – always a good sign.

N68 Bistro

2 Beaufort Arms Court
Monmouth
NP25 3UA
Tel: 01600 772055
https://www.facebook.com/N68Bistro

This bistro offers traditional British cuisine with a flair. Run by a mother and sons trio, their menu changes weekly (and is posted on their Facebook page), but you can always depend on them using the freshest ingredients grown or raised nearby. Everything on the menu is under £10 with the exception of the lamb – good prices for delicious dishes.

Shangri-La

17 Mary Street
Chepstow
Tel: 01291 622959

This restaurant is considered by many to offer the best Chinese food in Chepstow and environs. Its menu includes many familiar dishes, but offers enough deviation from the typical Chinese menu to excite foodies looking to try something new. Due to its popularity, it's likely to be packed when you visit, but the staff is welcoming and will seat you quickly.

Places to Shop

Eastgate Shopping Centre

Eastgate Street
Gloucester
http://intoeastgate.co.uk/home

Eastgate Street is a charming, brick-lane pedestrian thoroughfare that is lined with shops of all sorts. It's shopping centre will meet your needs for clothing, electronics and other goods.

Here you'll find M&S as well as cafes, bakeries and a food court. There is also a large, more traditional indoor market within the shopping centre where you'll find stalls set up by local artisans and foodmongers of various sorts so if the big name stores are not what you're looking for, the market will provide an interesting alternative.

Stella Books

Monmouth Road
Tintern
NP16 6SE
Tel: 01291 689755
http://www.stellabooks.com/

Stella Books is a specialty bookstore dedicated to rare books. Their shelves and storerooms house over 30,000 out-of-print tomes on every subject that range in price from £5 to £25,000. An easy stop to make after your visit to Tintern Abbey – at which point you might be interested in a book on local history. They've got a first edition *A Walk Through Wales in 1797* for £180 or, if that's out of your budget, you could opt for *Gwent Local History* (1982) for £5.

Labels Outlet Shopping

Ross-on-Wye, M50/J4, Herefordshire, HR9 7QQ
Tel: 01989 769000
http://www.labelsoutletshopping.co.uk/

Labels Outlet Shopping draws over a million visitors every year who come for the 200-plus brand names at bargain prices. You'll find all the brands you're familiar with and many smaller labels that you might not have heard of. For this reason, there isn't the kind of cookie-cutter sameness that you might find at other shopping centres. There is an excellent food hall on site – and for any dish you try, you can purchase the ingredients and recipe right there!

Ross Garden Store

Ross-on-Wye, Herefordshire, HR9 7BW
Tel: 01989 568999
http://www.rossgardenstore.com/

Spending all this time in such lush, beautiful outdoor settings is sure to inspire your green thumb. Whether you're a gardening novice or master horticulturist, a stop at the Ross Garden Store is sure to please. It's housed in what used to be a train yard, but today is practically a park of its own. The staff is able to help you locate whichever of the thousands of plants you might be looking for, and what they don't have they'll be happy to order for you. They also sell furniture and statuary to help accent your garden and give it character.

Gloucestershire Arts & Crafts Centre

4 College Street
Gloucester
GL1 2LE
Tel: 01452 307161
http://www.glosartscrafts.co.uk/

The Gloucestershire Arts and Crafts Centre is conveniently located beside the Cathedral. This collective is run by the artists who have made the pieces and products on sale, and you'll have the opportunity to speak with some of the artists themselves. With jewelry, tapestry, wall hangings, and a huge assortment of *objets d'art*, you'll find a wonderful range of unique pieces to peruse.

Printed in Great Britain
by Amazon.co.uk, Ltd.,
Marston Gate.